CHILD CUSTODY JOURNAL

DATES COVERED:
JOURNAL KEPT BY:
CHILD(REN)'S NAMES:

Child Custody Journal © 2019 Sosha Publishing
All rights reserved. No part of this book may be used or reproduced in any many whatsoever without written permissions except in the case of brief quotations embodied in reviews.
First Edition: 2019

Going through a divorce is a difficult process which becomes even more complicated when it involves the custody of your children.

Documenting everything – good, bad and neutral – can be extremely important when it comes to court or mediation in a child custody battle. Record everything as it happens, while your memory is sharp, and never lie or falsify details. This is about what is best for your child.

This journal is organized to record the details of all communication and visitation, with a section in the back for any additional notes. Be sure to include any comments made by your child or others, any signs of neglect or harm, any changes in your child's mood and behavior or performance in school, and anything else that you feel is important.

Be sure to discuss your documenting plans with your attorney to determine any additional types of information they feel would be helpful. This journal is intended to be an organizational tool; it should not be construed as legal advice in any way. Sosha Publishing and its employees are not attorneys.

VISITATION SCHEDULE

DATE	PICK UP		DROP OFF	
	TIME	LOCATION	TIME	LOCATION

VISITATION SCHEDULE

DATE	PICK UP		DROP OFF	
	TIME	LOCATION	TIME	LOCATION

VISITATION RECORD

PICK UP

DATE	AGREED TIME	ACTUAL TIME	LOCATION	PICKED UP BY

SPECIAL INSTRUCTIONS GIVEN:

CHILD(REN)'S REACTIONS:

NOTES:

DROP OFF

DATE	AGREED TIME	ACTUAL TIME	LOCATION	DROPPED OFF BY

CHILD(REN)'S PHYSICAL CONDITION:

CHILD(REN)'S REACTIONS:

NOTES:

VISITATION RECORD

PICK UP

DATE	AGREED TIME	ACTUAL TIME	LOCATION	PICKED UP BY

SPECIAL INSTRUCTIONS GIVEN:

CHILD(REN)'S REACTIONS:

NOTES:

DROP OFF

DATE	AGREED TIME	ACTUAL TIME	LOCATION	DROPPED OFF BY

CHILD(REN)'S PHYSICAL CONDITION:

CHILD(REN)'S REACTIONS:

NOTES:

VISITATION RECORD

PICK UP

DATE	AGREED TIME	ACTUAL TIME	LOCATION	PICKED UP BY

SPECIAL INSTRUCTIONS GIVEN:

CHILD(REN)'S REACTIONS:

NOTES:

DROP OFF

DATE	AGREED TIME	ACTUAL TIME	LOCATION	DROPPED OFF BY

CHILD(REN)'S PHYSICAL CONDITION:

CHILD(REN)'S REACTIONS:

NOTES:

VISITATION RECORD

PICK UP

DATE	AGREED TIME	ACTUAL TIME	LOCATION	PICKED UP BY

SPECIAL INSTRUCTIONS GIVEN:

CHILD(REN)'S REACTIONS:

NOTES:

DROP OFF

DATE	AGREED TIME	ACTUAL TIME	LOCATION	DROPPED OFF BY

CHILD(REN)'S PHYSICAL CONDITION:

CHILD(REN)'S REACTIONS:

NOTES:

VISITATION RECORD

PICK UP

DATE	AGREED TIME	ACTUAL TIME	LOCATION	PICKED UP BY

SPECIAL INSTRUCTIONS GIVEN:

CHILD(REN)'S REACTIONS:

NOTES:

DROP OFF

DATE	AGREED TIME	ACTUAL TIME	LOCATION	DROPPED OFF BY

CHILD(REN)'S PHYSICAL CONDITION:

CHILD(REN)'S REACTIONS:

NOTES:

VISITATION RECORD

PICK UP

DATE	AGREED TIME	ACTUAL TIME	LOCATION	PICKED UP BY

SPECIAL INSTRUCTIONS GIVEN:

CHILD(REN)'S REACTIONS:

NOTES:

DROP OFF

DATE	AGREED TIME	ACTUAL TIME	LOCATION	DROPPED OFF BY

CHILD(REN)'S PHYSICAL CONDITION:

CHILD(REN)'S REACTIONS:

NOTES:

VISITATION RECORD

PICK UP

DATE	AGREED TIME	ACTUAL TIME	LOCATION	PICKED UP BY

SPECIAL INSTRUCTIONS GIVEN:

CHILD(REN)'S REACTIONS:

NOTES:

DROP OFF

DATE	AGREED TIME	ACTUAL TIME	LOCATION	DROPPED OFF BY

CHILD(REN)'S PHYSICAL CONDITION:

CHILD(REN)'S REACTIONS:

NOTES:

VISITATION RECORD

		PICK UP		
DATE	**AGREED TIME**	**ACTUAL TIME**	**LOCATION**	**PICKED UP BY**

SPECIAL INSTRUCTIONS GIVEN:

CHILD(REN)'S REACTIONS:

NOTES:

		DROP OFF		
DATE	**AGREED TIME**	**ACTUAL TIME**	**LOCATION**	**DROPPED OFF BY**

CHILD(REN)'S PHYSICAL CONDITION:

CHILD(REN)'S REACTIONS:

NOTES:

VISITATION RECORD

PICK UP

DATE	AGREED TIME	ACTUAL TIME	LOCATION	PICKED UP BY

SPECIAL INSTRUCTIONS GIVEN:

CHILD(REN)'S REACTIONS:

NOTES:

DROP OFF

DATE	AGREED TIME	ACTUAL TIME	LOCATION	DROPPED OFF BY

CHILD(REN)'S PHYSICAL CONDITION:

CHILD(REN)'S REACTIONS:

NOTES:

VISITATION RECORD

PICK UP

DATE	AGREED TIME	ACTUAL TIME	LOCATION	PICKED UP BY

SPECIAL INSTRUCTIONS GIVEN:

CHILD(REN)'S REACTIONS:

NOTES:

DROP OFF

DATE	AGREED TIME	ACTUAL TIME	LOCATION	DROPPED OFF BY

CHILD(REN)'S PHYSICAL CONDITION:

CHILD(REN)'S REACTIONS:

NOTES:

VISITATION RECORD

PICK UP

DATE	AGREED TIME	ACTUAL TIME	LOCATION	PICKED UP BY

SPECIAL INSTRUCTIONS GIVEN:

CHILD(REN)'S REACTIONS:

NOTES:

DROP OFF

DATE	AGREED TIME	ACTUAL TIME	LOCATION	DROPPED OFF BY

CHILD(REN)'S PHYSICAL CONDITION:

CHILD(REN)'S REACTIONS:

NOTES:

VISITATION RECORD

PICK UP

DATE	AGREED TIME	ACTUAL TIME	LOCATION	PICKED UP BY

SPECIAL INSTRUCTIONS GIVEN:

CHILD(REN)'S REACTIONS:

NOTES:

DROP OFF

DATE	AGREED TIME	ACTUAL TIME	LOCATION	DROPPED OFF BY

CHILD(REN)'S PHYSICAL CONDITION:

CHILD(REN)'S REACTIONS:

NOTES:

VISITATION RECORD

PICK UP

DATE	AGREED TIME	ACTUAL TIME	LOCATION	PICKED UP BY

SPECIAL INSTRUCTIONS GIVEN:

CHILD(REN)'S REACTIONS:

NOTES:

DROP OFF

DATE	AGREED TIME	ACTUAL TIME	LOCATION	DROPPED OFF BY

CHILD(REN)'S PHYSICAL CONDITION:

CHILD(REN)'S REACTIONS:

NOTES:

VISITATION RECORD

PICK UP

DATE	AGREED TIME	ACTUAL TIME	LOCATION	PICKED UP BY

SPECIAL INSTRUCTIONS GIVEN:

CHILD(REN)'S REACTIONS:

NOTES:

DROP OFF

DATE	AGREED TIME	ACTUAL TIME	LOCATION	DROPPED OFF BY

CHILD(REN)'S PHYSICAL CONDITION:

CHILD(REN)'S REACTIONS:

NOTES:

VISITATION RECORD

PICK UP

DATE	AGREED TIME	ACTUAL TIME	LOCATION	PICKED UP BY

SPECIAL INSTRUCTIONS GIVEN:

CHILD(REN)'S REACTIONS:

NOTES:

DROP OFF

DATE	AGREED TIME	ACTUAL TIME	LOCATION	DROPPED OFF BY

CHILD(REN)'S PHYSICAL CONDITION:

CHILD(REN)'S REACTIONS:

NOTES:

VISITATION RECORD

PICK UP

DATE	AGREED TIME	ACTUAL TIME	LOCATION	PICKED UP BY

SPECIAL INSTRUCTIONS GIVEN:

CHILD(REN)'S REACTIONS:

NOTES:

DROP OFF

DATE	AGREED TIME	ACTUAL TIME	LOCATION	DROPPED OFF BY

CHILD(REN)'S PHYSICAL CONDITION:

CHILD(REN)'S REACTIONS:

NOTES:

VISITATION RECORD

PICK UP

DATE	AGREED TIME	ACTUAL TIME	LOCATION	PICKED UP BY

SPECIAL INSTRUCTIONS GIVEN:

CHILD(REN)'S REACTIONS:

NOTES:

DROP OFF

DATE	AGREED TIME	ACTUAL TIME	LOCATION	DROPPED OFF BY

CHILD(REN)'S PHYSICAL CONDITION:

CHILD(REN)'S REACTIONS:

NOTES:

VISITATION RECORD

PICK UP

DATE	AGREED TIME	ACTUAL TIME	LOCATION	PICKED UP BY

SPECIAL INSTRUCTIONS GIVEN:

CHILD(REN)'S REACTIONS:

NOTES:

DROP OFF

DATE	AGREED TIME	ACTUAL TIME	LOCATION	DROPPED OFF BY

CHILD(REN)'S PHYSICAL CONDITION:

CHILD(REN)'S REACTIONS:

NOTES:

VISITATION RECORD

PICK UP

DATE	AGREED TIME	ACTUAL TIME	LOCATION	PICKED UP BY

SPECIAL INSTRUCTIONS GIVEN:

CHILD(REN)'S REACTIONS:

NOTES:

DROP OFF

DATE	AGREED TIME	ACTUAL TIME	LOCATION	DROPPED OFF BY

CHILD(REN)'S PHYSICAL CONDITION:

CHILD(REN)'S REACTIONS:

NOTES:

VISITATION RECORD

PICK UP

DATE	AGREED TIME	ACTUAL TIME	LOCATION	PICKED UP BY

SPECIAL INSTRUCTIONS GIVEN:

CHILD(REN)'S REACTIONS:

NOTES:

DROP OFF

DATE	AGREED TIME	ACTUAL TIME	LOCATION	DROPPED OFF BY

CHILD(REN)'S PHYSICAL CONDITION:

CHILD(REN)'S REACTIONS:

NOTES:

VISITATION RECORD

PICK UP

DATE	AGREED TIME	ACTUAL TIME	LOCATION	PICKED UP BY

SPECIAL INSTRUCTIONS GIVEN:

CHILD(REN)'S REACTIONS:

NOTES:

DROP OFF

DATE	AGREED TIME	ACTUAL TIME	LOCATION	DROPPED OFF BY

CHILD(REN)'S PHYSICAL CONDITION:

CHILD(REN)'S REACTIONS:

NOTES:

VISITATION RECORD

PICK UP					
DATE	AGREED TIME	ACTUAL TIME	LOCATION	PICKED UP BY

SPECIAL INSTRUCTIONS GIVEN:

CHILD(REN)'S REACTIONS:

NOTES:

DROP OFF					
DATE	AGREED TIME	ACTUAL TIME	LOCATION	DROPPED OFF BY

CHILD(REN)'S PHYSICAL CONDITION:

CHILD(REN)'S REACTIONS:

NOTES:

VISITATION RECORD

PICK UP

DATE	AGREED TIME	ACTUAL TIME	LOCATION	PICKED UP BY

SPECIAL INSTRUCTIONS GIVEN:

CHILD(REN)'S REACTIONS:

NOTES:

DROP OFF

DATE	AGREED TIME	ACTUAL TIME	LOCATION	DROPPED OFF BY

CHILD(REN)'S PHYSICAL CONDITION:

CHILD(REN)'S REACTIONS:

NOTES:

VISITATION RECORD

PICK UP

DATE	AGREED TIME	ACTUAL TIME	LOCATION	PICKED UP BY

SPECIAL INSTRUCTIONS GIVEN:

CHILD(REN)'S REACTIONS:

NOTES:

DROP OFF

DATE	AGREED TIME	ACTUAL TIME	LOCATION	DROPPED OFF BY

CHILD(REN)'S PHYSICAL CONDITION:

CHILD(REN)'S REACTIONS:

NOTES:

VISITATION RECORD

PICK UP

DATE	AGREED TIME	ACTUAL TIME	LOCATION	PICKED UP BY

SPECIAL INSTRUCTIONS GIVEN:

CHILD(REN)'S REACTIONS:

NOTES:

DROP OFF

DATE	AGREED TIME	ACTUAL TIME	LOCATION	DROPPED OFF BY

CHILD(REN)'S PHYSICAL CONDITION:

CHILD(REN)'S REACTIONS:

NOTES:

VISITATION RECORD

PICK UP

DATE	AGREED TIME	ACTUAL TIME	LOCATION	PICKED UP BY

SPECIAL INSTRUCTIONS GIVEN:

CHILD(REN)'S REACTIONS:

NOTES:

DROP OFF

DATE	AGREED TIME	ACTUAL TIME	LOCATION	DROPPED OFF BY

CHILD(REN)'S PHYSICAL CONDITION:

CHILD(REN)'S REACTIONS:

NOTES:

VISITATION RECORD

PICK UP

DATE	AGREED TIME	ACTUAL TIME	LOCATION	PICKED UP BY

SPECIAL INSTRUCTIONS GIVEN:

CHILD(REN)'S REACTIONS:

NOTES:

DROP OFF

DATE	AGREED TIME	ACTUAL TIME	LOCATION	DROPPED OFF BY

CHILD(REN)'S PHYSICAL CONDITION:

CHILD(REN)'S REACTIONS:

NOTES:

VISITATION RECORD

			PICK UP	
DATE	**AGREED TIME**	**ACTUAL TIME**	**LOCATION**	**PICKED UP BY**

SPECIAL INSTRUCTIONS GIVEN:

CHILD(REN)'S REACTIONS:

NOTES:

			DROP OFF	
DATE	**AGREED TIME**	**ACTUAL TIME**	**LOCATION**	**DROPPED OFF BY**

CHILD(REN)'S PHYSICAL CONDITION:

CHILD(REN)'S REACTIONS:

NOTES:

VISITATION RECORD

PICK UP

DATE	AGREED TIME	ACTUAL TIME	LOCATION	PICKED UP BY

SPECIAL INSTRUCTIONS GIVEN:

CHILD(REN)'S REACTIONS:

NOTES:

DROP OFF

DATE	AGREED TIME	ACTUAL TIME	LOCATION	DROPPED OFF BY

CHILD(REN)'S PHYSICAL CONDITION:

CHILD(REN)'S REACTIONS:

NOTES:

VISITATION RECORD

PICK UP

DATE	AGREED TIME	ACTUAL TIME	LOCATION	PICKED UP BY

SPECIAL INSTRUCTIONS GIVEN:

CHILD(REN)'S REACTIONS:

NOTES:

DROP OFF

DATE	AGREED TIME	ACTUAL TIME	LOCATION	DROPPED OFF BY

CHILD(REN)'S PHYSICAL CONDITION:

CHILD(REN)'S REACTIONS:

NOTES:

VISITATION RECORD

PICK UP

DATE	AGREED TIME	ACTUAL TIME	LOCATION	PICKED UP BY

SPECIAL INSTRUCTIONS GIVEN:

CHILD(REN)'S REACTIONS:

NOTES:

DROP OFF

DATE	AGREED TIME	ACTUAL TIME	LOCATION	DROPPED OFF BY

CHILD(REN)'S PHYSICAL CONDITION:

CHILD(REN)'S REACTIONS:

NOTES:

VISITATION RECORD

		PICK UP		
DATE	AGREED TIME	ACTUAL TIME	LOCATION	PICKED UP BY

SPECIAL INSTRUCTIONS GIVEN:

CHILD(REN)'S REACTIONS:

NOTES:

		DROP OFF		
DATE	AGREED TIME	ACTUAL TIME	LOCATION	DROPPED OFF BY

CHILD(REN)'S PHYSICAL CONDITION:

CHILD(REN)'S REACTIONS:

NOTES:

VISITATION RECORD

PICK UP

DATE	AGREED TIME	ACTUAL TIME	LOCATION	PICKED UP BY

SPECIAL INSTRUCTIONS GIVEN:

CHILD(REN)'S REACTIONS:

NOTES:

DROP OFF

DATE	AGREED TIME	ACTUAL TIME	LOCATION	DROPPED OFF BY

CHILD(REN)'S PHYSICAL CONDITION:

CHILD(REN)'S REACTIONS:

NOTES:

VISITATION RECORD

PICK UP

DATE	AGREED TIME	ACTUAL TIME	LOCATION	PICKED UP BY

SPECIAL INSTRUCTIONS GIVEN:

CHILD(REN)'S REACTIONS:

NOTES:

DROP OFF

DATE	AGREED TIME	ACTUAL TIME	LOCATION	DROPPED OFF BY

CHILD(REN)'S PHYSICAL CONDITION:

CHILD(REN)'S REACTIONS:

NOTES:

VISITATION RECORD

PICK UP

DATE	AGREED TIME	ACTUAL TIME	LOCATION	PICKED UP BY

SPECIAL INSTRUCTIONS GIVEN:

CHILD(REN)'S REACTIONS:

NOTES:

DROP OFF

DATE	AGREED TIME	ACTUAL TIME	LOCATION	DROPPED OFF BY

CHILD(REN)'S PHYSICAL CONDITION:

CHILD(REN)'S REACTIONS:

NOTES:

VISITATION RECORD

PICK UP

DATE	AGREED TIME	ACTUAL TIME	LOCATION	PICKED UP BY

SPECIAL INSTRUCTIONS GIVEN:

CHILD(REN)'S REACTIONS:

NOTES:

DROP OFF

DATE	AGREED TIME	ACTUAL TIME	LOCATION	DROPPED OFF BY

CHILD(REN)'S PHYSICAL CONDITION:

CHILD(REN)'S REACTIONS:

NOTES:

VISITATION RECORD

PICK UP

DATE	AGREED TIME	ACTUAL TIME	LOCATION	PICKED UP BY

SPECIAL INSTRUCTIONS GIVEN:

CHILD(REN)'S REACTIONS:

NOTES:

DROP OFF

DATE	AGREED TIME	ACTUAL TIME	LOCATION	DROPPED OFF BY

CHILD(REN)'S PHYSICAL CONDITION:

CHILD(REN)'S REACTIONS:

NOTES:

VISITATION RECORD

PICK UP

DATE	AGREED TIME	ACTUAL TIME	LOCATION	PICKED UP BY

SPECIAL INSTRUCTIONS GIVEN:

CHILD(REN)'S REACTIONS:

NOTES:

DROP OFF

DATE	AGREED TIME	ACTUAL TIME	LOCATION	DROPPED OFF BY

CHILD(REN)'S PHYSICAL CONDITION:

CHILD(REN)'S REACTIONS:

NOTES:

VISITATION RECORD

PICK UP

DATE	AGREED TIME	ACTUAL TIME	LOCATION	PICKED UP BY

SPECIAL INSTRUCTIONS GIVEN:

CHILD(REN)'S REACTIONS:

NOTES:

DROP OFF

DATE	AGREED TIME	ACTUAL TIME	LOCATION	DROPPED OFF BY

CHILD(REN)'S PHYSICAL CONDITION:

CHILD(REN)'S REACTIONS:

NOTES:

VISITATION RECORD

PICK UP

DATE	AGREED TIME	ACTUAL TIME	LOCATION	PICKED UP BY

SPECIAL INSTRUCTIONS GIVEN:

CHILD(REN)'S REACTIONS:

NOTES:

DROP OFF

DATE	AGREED TIME	ACTUAL TIME	LOCATION	DROPPED OFF BY

CHILD(REN)'S PHYSICAL CONDITION:

CHILD(REN)'S REACTIONS:

NOTES:

VISITATION RECORD

PICK UP

DATE	AGREED TIME	ACTUAL TIME	LOCATION	PICKED UP BY

SPECIAL INSTRUCTIONS GIVEN:

CHILD(REN)'S REACTIONS:

NOTES:

DROP OFF

DATE	AGREED TIME	ACTUAL TIME	LOCATION	DROPPED OFF BY

CHILD(REN)'S PHYSICAL CONDITION:

CHILD(REN)'S REACTIONS:

NOTES:

VISITATION RECORD

PICK UP

DATE	AGREED TIME	ACTUAL TIME	LOCATION	PICKED UP BY

SPECIAL INSTRUCTIONS GIVEN:

CHILD(REN)'S REACTIONS:

NOTES:

DROP OFF

DATE	AGREED TIME	ACTUAL TIME	LOCATION	DROPPED OFF BY

CHILD(REN)'S PHYSICAL CONDITION:

CHILD(REN)'S REACTIONS:

NOTES:

VISITATION RECORD

PICK UP

DATE	AGREED TIME	ACTUAL TIME	LOCATION	PICKED UP BY

SPECIAL INSTRUCTIONS GIVEN:

CHILD(REN)'S REACTIONS:

NOTES:

DROP OFF

DATE	AGREED TIME	ACTUAL TIME	LOCATION	DROPPED OFF BY

CHILD(REN)'S PHYSICAL CONDITION:

CHILD(REN)'S REACTIONS:

NOTES:

VISITATION RECORD

PICK UP

DATE	AGREED TIME	ACTUAL TIME	LOCATION	PICKED UP BY

SPECIAL INSTRUCTIONS GIVEN:

CHILD(REN)'S REACTIONS:

NOTES:

DROP OFF

DATE	AGREED TIME	ACTUAL TIME	LOCATION	DROPPED OFF BY

CHILD(REN)'S PHYSICAL CONDITION:

CHILD(REN)'S REACTIONS:

NOTES:

COMMUNICATIONS RECORD

DATE:	TIME:	LENGTH OF CONTACT:

TYPE OF CONTACT: ☐ PHONE ☐ TEXT ☐ VIDEO CALL ☐ E-MAIL ☐ OTHER

CONTACT BETWEEN:

CONTACT INITIATED BY:

REASON FOR CONTACT (SUBJECT):

CHILD(REN)'S REACTIONS:

NOTES:

DATE:	TIME:	LENGTH OF CONTACT:

TYPE OF CONTACT: ☐ PHONE ☐ TEXT ☐ VIDEO CALL ☐ E-MAIL ☐ OTHER

CONTACT BETWEEN:

CONTACT INITIATED BY:

REASON FOR CONTACT (SUBJECT):

CHILD(REN)'S REACTIONS:

NOTES:

COMMUNICATIONS RECORD

DATE:	TIME:	LENGTH OF CONTACT:

TYPE OF CONTACT: ☐ PHONE ☐ TEXT ☐ VIDEO CALL ☐ E-MAIL ☐ OTHER

CONTACT BETWEEN:

CONTACT INITIATED BY:

REASON FOR CONTACT (SUBJECT):

CHILD(REN)'S REACTIONS:

NOTES:

DATE:	TIME:	LENGTH OF CONTACT:

TYPE OF CONTACT: ☐ PHONE ☐ TEXT ☐ VIDEO CALL ☐ E-MAIL ☐ OTHER

CONTACT BETWEEN:

CONTACT INITIATED BY:

REASON FOR CONTACT (SUBJECT):

CHILD(REN)'S REACTIONS:

NOTES:

COMMUNICATIONS RECORD

DATE:	TIME:	LENGTH OF CONTACT:

TYPE OF CONTACT: ☐ PHONE ☐ TEXT ☐ VIDEO CALL ☐ E-MAIL ☐ OTHER

CONTACT BETWEEN:

CONTACT INITIATED BY:

REASON FOR CONTACT (SUBJECT):

CHILD(REN)'S REACTIONS:

NOTES:

DATE:	TIME:	LENGTH OF CONTACT:

TYPE OF CONTACT: ☐ PHONE ☐ TEXT ☐ VIDEO CALL ☐ E-MAIL ☐ OTHER

CONTACT BETWEEN:

CONTACT INITIATED BY:

REASON FOR CONTACT (SUBJECT):

CHILD(REN)'S REACTIONS:

NOTES:

COMMUNICATIONS RECORD

DATE:	TIME:	LENGTH OF CONTACT:

TYPE OF CONTACT: ☐ PHONE ☐ TEXT ☐ VIDEO CALL ☐ E-MAIL ☐ OTHER

CONTACT BETWEEN:

CONTACT INITIATED BY:

REASON FOR CONTACT (SUBJECT):

CHILD(REN)'S REACTIONS:

NOTES:

DATE:	TIME:	LENGTH OF CONTACT:

TYPE OF CONTACT: ☐ PHONE ☐ TEXT ☐ VIDEO CALL ☐ E-MAIL ☐ OTHER

CONTACT BETWEEN:

CONTACT INITIATED BY:

REASON FOR CONTACT (SUBJECT):

CHILD(REN)'S REACTIONS:

NOTES:

COMMUNICATIONS RECORD

DATE:	TIME:	LENGTH OF CONTACT:

TYPE OF CONTACT: ☐ PHONE ☐ TEXT ☐ VIDEO CALL ☐ E-MAIL ☐ OTHER

CONTACT BETWEEN:

CONTACT INITIATED BY:

REASON FOR CONTACT (SUBJECT):

CHILD(REN)'S REACTIONS:

NOTES:

DATE:	TIME:	LENGTH OF CONTACT:

TYPE OF CONTACT: ☐ PHONE ☐ TEXT ☐ VIDEO CALL ☐ E-MAIL ☐ OTHER

CONTACT BETWEEN:

CONTACT INITIATED BY:

REASON FOR CONTACT (SUBJECT):

CHILD(REN)'S REACTIONS:

NOTES:

COMMUNICATIONS RECORD

DATE:	TIME:	LENGTH OF CONTACT:

TYPE OF CONTACT: ☐ PHONE ☐ TEXT ☐ VIDEO CALL ☐ E-MAIL ☐ OTHER

CONTACT BETWEEN:

CONTACT INITIATED BY:

REASON FOR CONTACT (SUBJECT):

CHILD(REN)'S REACTIONS:

NOTES:

DATE:	TIME:	LENGTH OF CONTACT:

TYPE OF CONTACT: ☐ PHONE ☐ TEXT ☐ VIDEO CALL ☐ E-MAIL ☐ OTHER

CONTACT BETWEEN:

CONTACT INITIATED BY:

REASON FOR CONTACT (SUBJECT):

CHILD(REN)'S REACTIONS:

NOTES:

COMMUNICATIONS RECORD

DATE:	TIME:	LENGTH OF CONTACT:

TYPE OF CONTACT: ☐ PHONE ☐ TEXT ☐ VIDEO CALL ☐ E-MAIL ☐ OTHER

CONTACT BETWEEN:

CONTACT INITIATED BY:

REASON FOR CONTACT (SUBJECT):

CHILD(REN)'S REACTIONS:

NOTES:

DATE:	TIME:	LENGTH OF CONTACT:

TYPE OF CONTACT: ☐ PHONE ☐ TEXT ☐ VIDEO CALL ☐ E-MAIL ☐ OTHER

CONTACT BETWEEN:

CONTACT INITIATED BY:

REASON FOR CONTACT (SUBJECT):

CHILD(REN)'S REACTIONS:

NOTES:

COMMUNICATIONS RECORD

DATE:	TIME:	LENGTH OF CONTACT:

TYPE OF CONTACT: ☐ PHONE ☐ TEXT ☐ VIDEO CALL ☐ E-MAIL ☐ OTHER

CONTACT BETWEEN:

CONTACT INITIATED BY:

REASON FOR CONTACT (SUBJECT):

CHILD(REN)'S REACTIONS:

NOTES:

DATE:	TIME:	LENGTH OF CONTACT:

TYPE OF CONTACT: ☐ PHONE ☐ TEXT ☐ VIDEO CALL ☐ E-MAIL ☐ OTHER

CONTACT BETWEEN:

CONTACT INITIATED BY:

REASON FOR CONTACT (SUBJECT):

CHILD(REN)'S REACTIONS:

NOTES:

COMMUNICATIONS RECORD

DATE:	TIME:	LENGTH OF CONTACT:

TYPE OF CONTACT: ☐ PHONE ☐ TEXT ☐ VIDEO CALL ☐ E-MAIL ☐ OTHER

CONTACT BETWEEN:

CONTACT INITIATED BY:

REASON FOR CONTACT (SUBJECT):

CHILD(REN)'S REACTIONS:

NOTES:

DATE:	TIME:	LENGTH OF CONTACT:

TYPE OF CONTACT: ☐ PHONE ☐ TEXT ☐ VIDEO CALL ☐ E-MAIL ☐ OTHER

CONTACT BETWEEN:

CONTACT INITIATED BY:

REASON FOR CONTACT (SUBJECT):

CHILD(REN)'S REACTIONS:

NOTES:

COMMUNICATIONS RECORD

DATE:	TIME:	LENGTH OF CONTACT:

TYPE OF CONTACT: ☐ PHONE ☐ TEXT ☐ VIDEO CALL ☐ E-MAIL ☐ OTHER

CONTACT BETWEEN:

CONTACT INITIATED BY:

REASON FOR CONTACT (SUBJECT):

CHILD(REN)'S REACTIONS:

NOTES:

DATE:	TIME:	LENGTH OF CONTACT:

TYPE OF CONTACT: ☐ PHONE ☐ TEXT ☐ VIDEO CALL ☐ E-MAIL ☐ OTHER

CONTACT BETWEEN:

CONTACT INITIATED BY:

REASON FOR CONTACT (SUBJECT):

CHILD(REN)'S REACTIONS:

NOTES:

COMMUNICATIONS RECORD

DATE:	TIME:	LENGTH OF CONTACT:

TYPE OF CONTACT: ☐ PHONE ☐ TEXT ☐ VIDEO CALL ☐ E-MAIL ☐ OTHER

CONTACT BETWEEN:

CONTACT INITIATED BY:

REASON FOR CONTACT (SUBJECT):

CHILD(REN)'S REACTIONS:

NOTES:

DATE:	TIME:	LENGTH OF CONTACT:

TYPE OF CONTACT: ☐ PHONE ☐ TEXT ☐ VIDEO CALL ☐ E-MAIL ☐ OTHER

CONTACT BETWEEN:

CONTACT INITIATED BY:

REASON FOR CONTACT (SUBJECT):

CHILD(REN)'S REACTIONS:

NOTES:

COMMUNICATIONS RECORD

DATE:	TIME:	LENGTH OF CONTACT:

TYPE OF CONTACT: ☐ PHONE ☐ TEXT ☐ VIDEO CALL ☐ E-MAIL ☐ OTHER

CONTACT BETWEEN:

CONTACT INITIATED BY:

REASON FOR CONTACT (SUBJECT):

CHILD(REN)'S REACTIONS:

NOTES:

DATE:	TIME:	LENGTH OF CONTACT:

TYPE OF CONTACT: ☐ PHONE ☐ TEXT ☐ VIDEO CALL ☐ E-MAIL ☐ OTHER

CONTACT BETWEEN:

CONTACT INITIATED BY:

REASON FOR CONTACT (SUBJECT):

CHILD(REN)'S REACTIONS:

NOTES:

COMMUNICATIONS RECORD

DATE:	TIME:	LENGTH OF CONTACT:

TYPE OF CONTACT: ☐ PHONE ☐ TEXT ☐ VIDEO CALL ☐ E-MAIL ☐ OTHER

CONTACT BETWEEN:

CONTACT INITIATED BY:

REASON FOR CONTACT (SUBJECT):

CHILD(REN)'S REACTIONS:

NOTES:

DATE:	TIME:	LENGTH OF CONTACT:

TYPE OF CONTACT: ☐ PHONE ☐ TEXT ☐ VIDEO CALL ☐ E-MAIL ☐ OTHER

CONTACT BETWEEN:

CONTACT INITIATED BY:

REASON FOR CONTACT (SUBJECT):

CHILD(REN)'S REACTIONS:

NOTES:

COMMUNICATIONS RECORD

DATE:	TIME:	LENGTH OF CONTACT:

TYPE OF CONTACT: ☐ PHONE ☐ TEXT ☐ VIDEO CALL ☐ E-MAIL ☐ OTHER

CONTACT BETWEEN:

CONTACT INITIATED BY:

REASON FOR CONTACT (SUBJECT):

CHILD(REN)'S REACTIONS:

NOTES:

DATE:	TIME:	LENGTH OF CONTACT:

TYPE OF CONTACT: ☐ PHONE ☐ TEXT ☐ VIDEO CALL ☐ E-MAIL ☐ OTHER

CONTACT BETWEEN:

CONTACT INITIATED BY:

REASON FOR CONTACT (SUBJECT):

CHILD(REN)'S REACTIONS:

NOTES:

COMMUNICATIONS RECORD

DATE:	TIME:	LENGTH OF CONTACT:

TYPE OF CONTACT: ☐ PHONE ☐ TEXT ☐ VIDEO CALL ☐ E-MAIL ☐ OTHER

CONTACT BETWEEN:

CONTACT INITIATED BY:

REASON FOR CONTACT (SUBJECT):

CHILD(REN)'S REACTIONS:

NOTES:

DATE:	TIME:	LENGTH OF CONTACT:

TYPE OF CONTACT: ☐ PHONE ☐ TEXT ☐ VIDEO CALL ☐ E-MAIL ☐ OTHER

CONTACT BETWEEN:

CONTACT INITIATED BY:

REASON FOR CONTACT (SUBJECT):

CHILD(REN)'S REACTIONS:

NOTES:

COMMUNICATIONS RECORD

DATE:	TIME:	LENGTH OF CONTACT:

TYPE OF CONTACT: ☐ PHONE ☐ TEXT ☐ VIDEO CALL ☐ E-MAIL ☐ OTHER

CONTACT BETWEEN:

CONTACT INITIATED BY:

REASON FOR CONTACT (SUBJECT):

CHILD(REN)'S REACTIONS:

NOTES:

DATE:	TIME:	LENGTH OF CONTACT:

TYPE OF CONTACT: ☐ PHONE ☐ TEXT ☐ VIDEO CALL ☐ E-MAIL ☐ OTHER

CONTACT BETWEEN:

CONTACT INITIATED BY:

REASON FOR CONTACT (SUBJECT):

CHILD(REN)'S REACTIONS:

NOTES:

COMMUNICATIONS RECORD

DATE:	TIME:	LENGTH OF CONTACT:

TYPE OF CONTACT: ☐ PHONE ☐ TEXT ☐ VIDEO CALL ☐ E-MAIL ☐ OTHER

CONTACT BETWEEN:

CONTACT INITIATED BY:

REASON FOR CONTACT (SUBJECT):

CHILD(REN)'S REACTIONS:

NOTES:

DATE:	TIME:	LENGTH OF CONTACT:

TYPE OF CONTACT: ☐ PHONE ☐ TEXT ☐ VIDEO CALL ☐ E-MAIL ☐ OTHER

CONTACT BETWEEN:

CONTACT INITIATED BY:

REASON FOR CONTACT (SUBJECT):

CHILD(REN)'S REACTIONS:

NOTES:

COMMUNICATIONS RECORD

DATE:	TIME:	LENGTH OF CONTACT:

TYPE OF CONTACT: ☐ PHONE ☐ TEXT ☐ VIDEO CALL ☐ E-MAIL ☐ OTHER

CONTACT BETWEEN:

CONTACT INITIATED BY:

REASON FOR CONTACT (SUBJECT):

CHILD(REN)'S REACTIONS:

NOTES:

DATE:	TIME:	LENGTH OF CONTACT:

TYPE OF CONTACT: ☐ PHONE ☐ TEXT ☐ VIDEO CALL ☐ E-MAIL ☐ OTHER

CONTACT BETWEEN:

CONTACT INITIATED BY:

REASON FOR CONTACT (SUBJECT):

CHILD(REN)'S REACTIONS:

NOTES:

COMMUNICATIONS RECORD

DATE:	TIME:	LENGTH OF CONTACT:

TYPE OF CONTACT: ☐ PHONE ☐ TEXT ☐ VIDEO CALL ☐ E-MAIL ☐ OTHER

CONTACT BETWEEN:

CONTACT INITIATED BY:

REASON FOR CONTACT (SUBJECT):

CHILD(REN)'S REACTIONS:

NOTES:

DATE:	TIME:	LENGTH OF CONTACT:

TYPE OF CONTACT: ☐ PHONE ☐ TEXT ☐ VIDEO CALL ☐ E-MAIL ☐ OTHER

CONTACT BETWEEN:

CONTACT INITIATED BY:

REASON FOR CONTACT (SUBJECT):

CHILD(REN)'S REACTIONS:

NOTES:

COMMUNICATIONS RECORD

DATE:	TIME:	LENGTH OF CONTACT:

TYPE OF CONTACT: ☐ PHONE ☐ TEXT ☐ VIDEO CALL ☐ E-MAIL ☐ OTHER

CONTACT BETWEEN:

CONTACT INITIATED BY:

REASON FOR CONTACT (SUBJECT):

CHILD(REN)'S REACTIONS:

NOTES:

DATE:	TIME:	LENGTH OF CONTACT:

TYPE OF CONTACT: ☐ PHONE ☐ TEXT ☐ VIDEO CALL ☐ E-MAIL ☐ OTHER

CONTACT BETWEEN:

CONTACT INITIATED BY:

REASON FOR CONTACT (SUBJECT):

CHILD(REN)'S REACTIONS:

NOTES:

COMMUNICATIONS RECORD

DATE:	TIME:	LENGTH OF CONTACT:

TYPE OF CONTACT: ☐ PHONE ☐ TEXT ☐ VIDEO CALL ☐ E-MAIL ☐ OTHER

CONTACT BETWEEN:

CONTACT INITIATED BY:

REASON FOR CONTACT (SUBJECT):

CHILD(REN)'S REACTIONS:

NOTES:

DATE:	TIME:	LENGTH OF CONTACT:

TYPE OF CONTACT: ☐ PHONE ☐ TEXT ☐ VIDEO CALL ☐ E-MAIL ☐ OTHER

CONTACT BETWEEN:

CONTACT INITIATED BY:

REASON FOR CONTACT (SUBJECT):

CHILD(REN)'S REACTIONS:

NOTES:

COMMUNICATIONS RECORD

DATE:	TIME:	LENGTH OF CONTACT:

TYPE OF CONTACT: ☐ PHONE ☐ TEXT ☐ VIDEO CALL ☐ E-MAIL ☐ OTHER

CONTACT BETWEEN:

CONTACT INITIATED BY:

REASON FOR CONTACT (SUBJECT):

CHILD(REN)'S REACTIONS:

NOTES:

DATE:	TIME:	LENGTH OF CONTACT:

TYPE OF CONTACT: ☐ PHONE ☐ TEXT ☐ VIDEO CALL ☐ E-MAIL ☐ OTHER

CONTACT BETWEEN:

CONTACT INITIATED BY:

REASON FOR CONTACT (SUBJECT):

CHILD(REN)'S REACTIONS:

NOTES:

COMMUNICATIONS RECORD

DATE:	TIME:	LENGTH OF CONTACT:

TYPE OF CONTACT: ☐ PHONE ☐ TEXT ☐ VIDEO CALL ☐ E-MAIL ☐ OTHER

CONTACT BETWEEN:

CONTACT INITIATED BY:

REASON FOR CONTACT (SUBJECT):

CHILD(REN)'S REACTIONS:

NOTES:

DATE:	TIME:	LENGTH OF CONTACT:

TYPE OF CONTACT: ☐ PHONE ☐ TEXT ☐ VIDEO CALL ☐ E-MAIL ☐ OTHER

CONTACT BETWEEN:

CONTACT INITIATED BY:

REASON FOR CONTACT (SUBJECT):

CHILD(REN)'S REACTIONS:

NOTES:

COMMUNICATIONS RECORD

DATE:	TIME:	LENGTH OF CONTACT:

TYPE OF CONTACT: ☐ PHONE ☐ TEXT ☐ VIDEO CALL ☐ E-MAIL ☐ OTHER

CONTACT BETWEEN:

CONTACT INITIATED BY:

REASON FOR CONTACT (SUBJECT):

CHILD(REN)'S REACTIONS:

NOTES:

DATE:	TIME:	LENGTH OF CONTACT:

TYPE OF CONTACT: ☐ PHONE ☐ TEXT ☐ VIDEO CALL ☐ E-MAIL ☐ OTHER

CONTACT BETWEEN:

CONTACT INITIATED BY:

REASON FOR CONTACT (SUBJECT):

CHILD(REN)'S REACTIONS:

NOTES:

COMMUNICATIONS RECORD

DATE:	TIME:	LENGTH OF CONTACT:

TYPE OF CONTACT: ☐ PHONE ☐ TEXT ☐ VIDEO CALL ☐ E-MAIL ☐ OTHER

CONTACT BETWEEN:

CONTACT INITIATED BY:

REASON FOR CONTACT (SUBJECT):

CHILD(REN)'S REACTIONS:

NOTES:

DATE:	TIME:	LENGTH OF CONTACT:

TYPE OF CONTACT: ☐ PHONE ☐ TEXT ☐ VIDEO CALL ☐ E-MAIL ☐ OTHER

CONTACT BETWEEN:

CONTACT INITIATED BY:

REASON FOR CONTACT (SUBJECT):

CHILD(REN)'S REACTIONS:

NOTES:

COMMUNICATIONS RECORD

DATE:	TIME:	LENGTH OF CONTACT:

TYPE OF CONTACT: ☐ PHONE ☐ TEXT ☐ VIDEO CALL ☐ E-MAIL ☐ OTHER

CONTACT BETWEEN:

CONTACT INITIATED BY:

REASON FOR CONTACT (SUBJECT):

CHILD(REN)'S REACTIONS:

NOTES:

DATE:	TIME:	LENGTH OF CONTACT:

TYPE OF CONTACT: ☐ PHONE ☐ TEXT ☐ VIDEO CALL ☐ E-MAIL ☐ OTHER

CONTACT BETWEEN:

CONTACT INITIATED BY:

REASON FOR CONTACT (SUBJECT):

CHILD(REN)'S REACTIONS:

NOTES:

COMMUNICATIONS RECORD

DATE:	TIME:	LENGTH OF CONTACT:

TYPE OF CONTACT: ☐ PHONE ☐ TEXT ☐ VIDEO CALL ☐ E-MAIL ☐ OTHER

CONTACT BETWEEN:

CONTACT INITIATED BY:

REASON FOR CONTACT (SUBJECT):

CHILD(REN)'S REACTIONS:

NOTES:

DATE:	TIME:	LENGTH OF CONTACT:

TYPE OF CONTACT: ☐ PHONE ☐ TEXT ☐ VIDEO CALL ☐ E-MAIL ☐ OTHER

CONTACT BETWEEN:

CONTACT INITIATED BY:

REASON FOR CONTACT (SUBJECT):

CHILD(REN)'S REACTIONS:

NOTES:

COMMUNICATIONS RECORD

DATE:	TIME:	LENGTH OF CONTACT:

TYPE OF CONTACT: ☐ PHONE ☐ TEXT ☐ VIDEO CALL ☐ E-MAIL ☐ OTHER

CONTACT BETWEEN:

CONTACT INITIATED BY:

REASON FOR CONTACT (SUBJECT):

CHILD(REN)'S REACTIONS:

NOTES:

DATE:	TIME:	LENGTH OF CONTACT:

TYPE OF CONTACT: ☐ PHONE ☐ TEXT ☐ VIDEO CALL ☐ E-MAIL ☐ OTHER

CONTACT BETWEEN:

CONTACT INITIATED BY:

REASON FOR CONTACT (SUBJECT):

CHILD(REN)'S REACTIONS:

NOTES:

COMMUNICATIONS RECORD

DATE:	TIME:	LENGTH OF CONTACT:

TYPE OF CONTACT: ☐ PHONE ☐ TEXT ☐ VIDEO CALL ☐ E-MAIL ☐ OTHER

CONTACT BETWEEN:

CONTACT INITIATED BY:

REASON FOR CONTACT (SUBJECT):

CHILD(REN)'S REACTIONS:

NOTES:

DATE:	TIME:	LENGTH OF CONTACT:

TYPE OF CONTACT: ☐ PHONE ☐ TEXT ☐ VIDEO CALL ☐ E-MAIL ☐ OTHER

CONTACT BETWEEN:

CONTACT INITIATED BY:

REASON FOR CONTACT (SUBJECT):

CHILD(REN)'S REACTIONS:

NOTES:

COMMUNICATIONS RECORD

DATE:	TIME:	LENGTH OF CONTACT:

TYPE OF CONTACT: ☐ PHONE ☐ TEXT ☐ VIDEO CALL ☐ E-MAIL ☐ OTHER

CONTACT BETWEEN:

CONTACT INITIATED BY:

REASON FOR CONTACT (SUBJECT):

CHILD(REN)'S REACTIONS:

NOTES:

DATE:	TIME:	LENGTH OF CONTACT:

TYPE OF CONTACT: ☐ PHONE ☐ TEXT ☐ VIDEO CALL ☐ E-MAIL ☐ OTHER

CONTACT BETWEEN:

CONTACT INITIATED BY:

REASON FOR CONTACT (SUBJECT):

CHILD(REN)'S REACTIONS:

NOTES:

COMMUNICATIONS RECORD

DATE:	TIME:	LENGTH OF CONTACT:

TYPE OF CONTACT: ☐ PHONE ☐ TEXT ☐ VIDEO CALL ☐ E-MAIL ☐ OTHER

CONTACT BETWEEN:

CONTACT INITIATED BY:

REASON FOR CONTACT (SUBJECT):

CHILD(REN)'S REACTIONS:

NOTES:

DATE:	TIME:	LENGTH OF CONTACT:

TYPE OF CONTACT: ☐ PHONE ☐ TEXT ☐ VIDEO CALL ☐ E-MAIL ☐ OTHER

CONTACT BETWEEN:

CONTACT INITIATED BY:

REASON FOR CONTACT (SUBJECT):

CHILD(REN)'S REACTIONS:

NOTES:

COMMUNICATIONS RECORD

DATE:	TIME:	LENGTH OF CONTACT:

TYPE OF CONTACT: ☐ PHONE ☐ TEXT ☐ VIDEO CALL ☐ E-MAIL ☐ OTHER

CONTACT BETWEEN:

CONTACT INITIATED BY:

REASON FOR CONTACT (SUBJECT):

CHILD(REN)'S REACTIONS:

NOTES:

DATE:	TIME:	LENGTH OF CONTACT:

TYPE OF CONTACT: ☐ PHONE ☐ TEXT ☐ VIDEO CALL ☐ E-MAIL ☐ OTHER

CONTACT BETWEEN:

CONTACT INITIATED BY:

REASON FOR CONTACT (SUBJECT):

CHILD(REN)'S REACTIONS:

NOTES:

COMMUNICATIONS RECORD

DATE:	TIME:	LENGTH OF CONTACT:

TYPE OF CONTACT: ☐ PHONE ☐ TEXT ☐ VIDEO CALL ☐ E-MAIL ☐ OTHER

CONTACT BETWEEN:

CONTACT INITIATED BY:

REASON FOR CONTACT (SUBJECT):

CHILD(REN)'S REACTIONS:

NOTES:

DATE:	TIME:	LENGTH OF CONTACT:

TYPE OF CONTACT: ☐ PHONE ☐ TEXT ☐ VIDEO CALL ☐ E-MAIL ☐ OTHER

CONTACT BETWEEN:

CONTACT INITIATED BY:

REASON FOR CONTACT (SUBJECT):

CHILD(REN)'S REACTIONS:

NOTES:

COMMUNICATIONS RECORD

DATE:	TIME:	LENGTH OF CONTACT:

TYPE OF CONTACT: ☐ PHONE ☐ TEXT ☐ VIDEO CALL ☐ E-MAIL ☐ OTHER

CONTACT BETWEEN:

CONTACT INITIATED BY:

REASON FOR CONTACT (SUBJECT):

CHILD(REN)'S REACTIONS:

NOTES:

DATE:	TIME:	LENGTH OF CONTACT:

TYPE OF CONTACT: ☐ PHONE ☐ TEXT ☐ VIDEO CALL ☐ E-MAIL ☐ OTHER

CONTACT BETWEEN:

CONTACT INITIATED BY:

REASON FOR CONTACT (SUBJECT):

CHILD(REN)'S REACTIONS:

NOTES:

COMMUNICATIONS RECORD

DATE:	TIME:	LENGTH OF CONTACT:

TYPE OF CONTACT: ☐ PHONE ☐ TEXT ☐ VIDEO CALL ☐ E-MAIL ☐ OTHER

CONTACT BETWEEN:

CONTACT INITIATED BY:

REASON FOR CONTACT (SUBJECT):

CHILD(REN)'S REACTIONS:

NOTES:

DATE:	TIME:	LENGTH OF CONTACT:

TYPE OF CONTACT: ☐ PHONE ☐ TEXT ☐ VIDEO CALL ☐ E-MAIL ☐ OTHER

CONTACT BETWEEN:

CONTACT INITIATED BY:

REASON FOR CONTACT (SUBJECT):

CHILD(REN)'S REACTIONS:

NOTES:

COMMUNICATIONS RECORD

DATE:	TIME:	LENGTH OF CONTACT:

TYPE OF CONTACT: ☐ PHONE ☐ TEXT ☐ VIDEO CALL ☐ E-MAIL ☐ OTHER

CONTACT BETWEEN:

CONTACT INITIATED BY:

REASON FOR CONTACT (SUBJECT):

CHILD(REN)'S REACTIONS:

NOTES:

DATE:	TIME:	LENGTH OF CONTACT:

TYPE OF CONTACT: ☐ PHONE ☐ TEXT ☐ VIDEO CALL ☐ E-MAIL ☐ OTHER

CONTACT BETWEEN:

CONTACT INITIATED BY:

REASON FOR CONTACT (SUBJECT):

CHILD(REN)'S REACTIONS:

NOTES:

COMMUNICATIONS RECORD

DATE:	TIME:	LENGTH OF CONTACT:

TYPE OF CONTACT: ☐ PHONE ☐ TEXT ☐ VIDEO CALL ☐ E-MAIL ☐ OTHER

CONTACT BETWEEN:

CONTACT INITIATED BY:

REASON FOR CONTACT (SUBJECT):

CHILD(REN)'S REACTIONS:

NOTES:

DATE:	TIME:	LENGTH OF CONTACT:

TYPE OF CONTACT: ☐ PHONE ☐ TEXT ☐ VIDEO CALL ☐ E-MAIL ☐ OTHER

CONTACT BETWEEN:

CONTACT INITIATED BY:

REASON FOR CONTACT (SUBJECT):

CHILD(REN)'S REACTIONS:

NOTES:

COMMUNICATIONS RECORD

DATE:	TIME:	LENGTH OF CONTACT:

TYPE OF CONTACT: ☐ PHONE ☐ TEXT ☐ VIDEO CALL ☐ E-MAIL ☐ OTHER

CONTACT BETWEEN:

CONTACT INITIATED BY:

REASON FOR CONTACT (SUBJECT):

CHILD(REN)'S REACTIONS:

NOTES:

DATE:	TIME:	LENGTH OF CONTACT:

TYPE OF CONTACT: ☐ PHONE ☐ TEXT ☐ VIDEO CALL ☐ E-MAIL ☐ OTHER

CONTACT BETWEEN:

CONTACT INITIATED BY:

REASON FOR CONTACT (SUBJECT):

CHILD(REN)'S REACTIONS:

NOTES:

COMMUNICATIONS RECORD

DATE:	TIME:	LENGTH OF CONTACT:

TYPE OF CONTACT: ☐ PHONE ☐ TEXT ☐ VIDEO CALL ☐ E-MAIL ☐ OTHER

CONTACT BETWEEN:

CONTACT INITIATED BY:

REASON FOR CONTACT (SUBJECT):

CHILD(REN)'S REACTIONS:

NOTES:

DATE:	TIME:	LENGTH OF CONTACT:

TYPE OF CONTACT: ☐ PHONE ☐ TEXT ☐ VIDEO CALL ☐ E-MAIL ☐ OTHER

CONTACT BETWEEN:

CONTACT INITIATED BY:

REASON FOR CONTACT (SUBJECT):

CHILD(REN)'S REACTIONS:

NOTES:

COMMUNICATIONS RECORD

DATE:	TIME:	LENGTH OF CONTACT:

TYPE OF CONTACT: ☐ PHONE ☐ TEXT ☐ VIDEO CALL ☐ E-MAIL ☐ OTHER

CONTACT BETWEEN:

CONTACT INITIATED BY:

REASON FOR CONTACT (SUBJECT):

CHILD(REN)'S REACTIONS:

NOTES:

DATE:	TIME:	LENGTH OF CONTACT:

TYPE OF CONTACT: ☐ PHONE ☐ TEXT ☐ VIDEO CALL ☐ E-MAIL ☐ OTHER

CONTACT BETWEEN:

CONTACT INITIATED BY:

REASON FOR CONTACT (SUBJECT):

CHILD(REN)'S REACTIONS:

NOTES:

COMMUNICATIONS RECORD

DATE:	TIME:	LENGTH OF CONTACT:

TYPE OF CONTACT: ☐ PHONE ☐ TEXT ☐ VIDEO CALL ☐ E-MAIL ☐ OTHER

CONTACT BETWEEN:

CONTACT INITIATED BY:

REASON FOR CONTACT (SUBJECT):

CHILD(REN)'S REACTIONS:

NOTES:

DATE:	TIME:	LENGTH OF CONTACT:

TYPE OF CONTACT: ☐ PHONE ☐ TEXT ☐ VIDEO CALL ☐ E-MAIL ☐ OTHER

CONTACT BETWEEN:

CONTACT INITIATED BY:

REASON FOR CONTACT (SUBJECT):

CHILD(REN)'S REACTIONS:

NOTES:

COMMUNICATIONS RECORD

DATE:	TIME:	LENGTH OF CONTACT:

TYPE OF CONTACT: ☐ PHONE ☐ TEXT ☐ VIDEO CALL ☐ E-MAIL ☐ OTHER

CONTACT BETWEEN:

CONTACT INITIATED BY:

REASON FOR CONTACT (SUBJECT):

CHILD(REN)'S REACTIONS:

NOTES:

DATE:	TIME:	LENGTH OF CONTACT:

TYPE OF CONTACT: ☐ PHONE ☐ TEXT ☐ VIDEO CALL ☐ E-MAIL ☐ OTHER

CONTACT BETWEEN:

CONTACT INITIATED BY:

REASON FOR CONTACT (SUBJECT):

CHILD(REN)'S REACTIONS:

NOTES:

COMMUNICATIONS RECORD

DATE:	TIME:	LENGTH OF CONTACT:

TYPE OF CONTACT: ☐ PHONE ☐ TEXT ☐ VIDEO CALL ☐ E-MAIL ☐ OTHER

CONTACT BETWEEN:

CONTACT INITIATED BY:

REASON FOR CONTACT (SUBJECT):

CHILD(REN)'S REACTIONS:

NOTES:

DATE:	TIME:	LENGTH OF CONTACT:

TYPE OF CONTACT: ☐ PHONE ☐ TEXT ☐ VIDEO CALL ☐ E-MAIL ☐ OTHER

CONTACT BETWEEN:

CONTACT INITIATED BY:

REASON FOR CONTACT (SUBJECT):

CHILD(REN)'S REACTIONS:

NOTES:

COMMUNICATIONS RECORD

DATE:	TIME:	LENGTH OF CONTACT:

TYPE OF CONTACT: ☐ PHONE ☐ TEXT ☐ VIDEO CALL ☐ E-MAIL ☐ OTHER

CONTACT BETWEEN:

CONTACT INITIATED BY:

REASON FOR CONTACT (SUBJECT):

CHILD(REN)'S REACTIONS:

NOTES:

DATE:	TIME:	LENGTH OF CONTACT:

TYPE OF CONTACT: ☐ PHONE ☐ TEXT ☐ VIDEO CALL ☐ E-MAIL ☐ OTHER

CONTACT BETWEEN:

CONTACT INITIATED BY:

REASON FOR CONTACT (SUBJECT):

CHILD(REN)'S REACTIONS:

NOTES:

COMMUNICATIONS RECORD

DATE:	TIME:	LENGTH OF CONTACT:

TYPE OF CONTACT: ☐ PHONE ☐ TEXT ☐ VIDEO CALL ☐ E-MAIL ☐ OTHER

CONTACT BETWEEN:

CONTACT INITIATED BY:

REASON FOR CONTACT (SUBJECT):

CHILD(REN)'S REACTIONS:

NOTES:

DATE:	TIME:	LENGTH OF CONTACT:

TYPE OF CONTACT: ☐ PHONE ☐ TEXT ☐ VIDEO CALL ☐ E-MAIL ☐ OTHER

CONTACT BETWEEN:

CONTACT INITIATED BY:

REASON FOR CONTACT (SUBJECT):

CHILD(REN)'S REACTIONS:

NOTES:

COMMUNICATIONS RECORD

DATE:	TIME:	LENGTH OF CONTACT:

TYPE OF CONTACT: ☐ PHONE ☐ TEXT ☐ VIDEO CALL ☐ E-MAIL ☐ OTHER

CONTACT BETWEEN:

CONTACT INITIATED BY:

REASON FOR CONTACT (SUBJECT):

CHILD(REN)'S REACTIONS:

NOTES:

DATE:	TIME:	LENGTH OF CONTACT:

TYPE OF CONTACT: ☐ PHONE ☐ TEXT ☐ VIDEO CALL ☐ E-MAIL ☐ OTHER

CONTACT BETWEEN:

CONTACT INITIATED BY:

REASON FOR CONTACT (SUBJECT):

CHILD(REN)'S REACTIONS:

NOTES:

COMMUNICATIONS RECORD

DATE:	TIME:	LENGTH OF CONTACT:

TYPE OF CONTACT: ☐ PHONE ☐ TEXT ☐ VIDEO CALL ☐ E-MAIL ☐ OTHER

CONTACT BETWEEN:

CONTACT INITIATED BY:

REASON FOR CONTACT (SUBJECT):

CHILD(REN)'S REACTIONS:

NOTES:

DATE:	TIME:	LENGTH OF CONTACT:

TYPE OF CONTACT: ☐ PHONE ☐ TEXT ☐ VIDEO CALL ☐ E-MAIL ☐ OTHER

CONTACT BETWEEN:

CONTACT INITIATED BY:

REASON FOR CONTACT (SUBJECT):

CHILD(REN)'S REACTIONS:

NOTES:

COMMUNICATIONS RECORD

DATE:	TIME:	LENGTH OF CONTACT:

TYPE OF CONTACT: ☐ PHONE ☐ TEXT ☐ VIDEO CALL ☐ E-MAIL ☐ OTHER

CONTACT BETWEEN:

CONTACT INITIATED BY:

REASON FOR CONTACT (SUBJECT):

CHILD(REN)'S REACTIONS:

NOTES:

DATE:	TIME:	LENGTH OF CONTACT:

TYPE OF CONTACT: ☐ PHONE ☐ TEXT ☐ VIDEO CALL ☐ E-MAIL ☐ OTHER

CONTACT BETWEEN:

CONTACT INITIATED BY:

REASON FOR CONTACT (SUBJECT):

CHILD(REN)'S REACTIONS:

NOTES:

COMMUNICATIONS RECORD

DATE:	TIME:	LENGTH OF CONTACT:

TYPE OF CONTACT: ☐ PHONE ☐ TEXT ☐ VIDEO CALL ☐ E-MAIL ☐ OTHER

CONTACT BETWEEN:

CONTACT INITIATED BY:

REASON FOR CONTACT (SUBJECT):

CHILD(REN)'S REACTIONS:

NOTES:

DATE:	TIME:	LENGTH OF CONTACT:

TYPE OF CONTACT: ☐ PHONE ☐ TEXT ☐ VIDEO CALL ☐ E-MAIL ☐ OTHER

CONTACT BETWEEN:

CONTACT INITIATED BY:

REASON FOR CONTACT (SUBJECT):

CHILD(REN)'S REACTIONS:

NOTES:

COMMUNICATIONS RECORD

DATE:	TIME:	LENGTH OF CONTACT:

TYPE OF CONTACT: ☐ PHONE ☐ TEXT ☐ VIDEO CALL ☐ E-MAIL ☐ OTHER

CONTACT BETWEEN:

CONTACT INITIATED BY:

REASON FOR CONTACT (SUBJECT):

CHILD(REN)'S REACTIONS:

NOTES:

DATE:	TIME:	LENGTH OF CONTACT:

TYPE OF CONTACT: ☐ PHONE ☐ TEXT ☐ VIDEO CALL ☐ E-MAIL ☐ OTHER

CONTACT BETWEEN:

CONTACT INITIATED BY:

REASON FOR CONTACT (SUBJECT):

CHILD(REN)'S REACTIONS:

NOTES:

COMMUNICATIONS RECORD

DATE:	TIME:	LENGTH OF CONTACT:

TYPE OF CONTACT: ☐ PHONE ☐ TEXT ☐ VIDEO CALL ☐ E-MAIL ☐ OTHER

CONTACT BETWEEN:

CONTACT INITIATED BY:

REASON FOR CONTACT (SUBJECT):

CHILD(REN)'S REACTIONS:

NOTES:

DATE:	TIME:	LENGTH OF CONTACT:

TYPE OF CONTACT: ☐ PHONE ☐ TEXT ☐ VIDEO CALL ☐ E-MAIL ☐ OTHER

CONTACT BETWEEN:

CONTACT INITIATED BY:

REASON FOR CONTACT (SUBJECT):

CHILD(REN)'S REACTIONS:

NOTES:

COMMUNICATIONS RECORD

DATE:	TIME:	LENGTH OF CONTACT:

TYPE OF CONTACT: ☐ PHONE ☐ TEXT ☐ VIDEO CALL ☐ E-MAIL ☐ OTHER

CONTACT BETWEEN:

CONTACT INITIATED BY:

REASON FOR CONTACT (SUBJECT):

CHILD(REN)'S REACTIONS:

NOTES:

DATE:	TIME:	LENGTH OF CONTACT:

TYPE OF CONTACT: ☐ PHONE ☐ TEXT ☐ VIDEO CALL ☐ E-MAIL ☐ OTHER

CONTACT BETWEEN:

CONTACT INITIATED BY:

REASON FOR CONTACT (SUBJECT):

CHILD(REN)'S REACTIONS:

NOTES:

COMMUNICATIONS RECORD

DATE:	TIME:	LENGTH OF CONTACT:

TYPE OF CONTACT: ☐ PHONE ☐ TEXT ☐ VIDEO CALL ☐ E-MAIL ☐ OTHER

CONTACT BETWEEN:

CONTACT INITIATED BY:

REASON FOR CONTACT (SUBJECT):

CHILD(REN)'S REACTIONS:

NOTES:

DATE:	TIME:	LENGTH OF CONTACT:

TYPE OF CONTACT: ☐ PHONE ☐ TEXT ☐ VIDEO CALL ☐ E-MAIL ☐ OTHER

CONTACT BETWEEN:

CONTACT INITIATED BY:

REASON FOR CONTACT (SUBJECT):

CHILD(REN)'S REACTIONS:

NOTES:

COMMUNICATIONS RECORD

DATE:	TIME:	LENGTH OF CONTACT:

TYPE OF CONTACT: ☐ PHONE ☐ TEXT ☐ VIDEO CALL ☐ E-MAIL ☐ OTHER

CONTACT BETWEEN:

CONTACT INITIATED BY:

REASON FOR CONTACT (SUBJECT):

CHILD(REN)'S REACTIONS:

NOTES:

DATE:	TIME:	LENGTH OF CONTACT:

TYPE OF CONTACT: ☐ PHONE ☐ TEXT ☐ VIDEO CALL ☐ E-MAIL ☐ OTHER

CONTACT BETWEEN:

CONTACT INITIATED BY:

REASON FOR CONTACT (SUBJECT):

CHILD(REN)'S REACTIONS:

NOTES:

COMMUNICATIONS RECORD

DATE:	TIME:	LENGTH OF CONTACT:

TYPE OF CONTACT: ☐ PHONE ☐ TEXT ☐ VIDEO CALL ☐ E-MAIL ☐ OTHER

CONTACT BETWEEN:

CONTACT INITIATED BY:

REASON FOR CONTACT (SUBJECT):

CHILD(REN)'S REACTIONS:

NOTES:

DATE:	TIME:	LENGTH OF CONTACT:

TYPE OF CONTACT: ☐ PHONE ☐ TEXT ☐ VIDEO CALL ☐ E-MAIL ☐ OTHER

CONTACT BETWEEN:

CONTACT INITIATED BY:

REASON FOR CONTACT (SUBJECT):

CHILD(REN)'S REACTIONS:

NOTES:

COMMUNICATIONS RECORD

DATE:	TIME:	LENGTH OF CONTACT:

TYPE OF CONTACT: ☐ PHONE ☐ TEXT ☐ VIDEO CALL ☐ E-MAIL ☐ OTHER

CONTACT BETWEEN:

CONTACT INITIATED BY:

REASON FOR CONTACT (SUBJECT):

CHILD(REN)'S REACTIONS:

NOTES:

DATE:	TIME:	LENGTH OF CONTACT:

TYPE OF CONTACT: ☐ PHONE ☐ TEXT ☐ VIDEO CALL ☐ E-MAIL ☐ OTHER

CONTACT BETWEEN:

CONTACT INITIATED BY:

REASON FOR CONTACT (SUBJECT):

CHILD(REN)'S REACTIONS:

NOTES:

COMMUNICATIONS RECORD

DATE:	TIME:	LENGTH OF CONTACT:

TYPE OF CONTACT: ☐ PHONE ☐ TEXT ☐ VIDEO CALL ☐ E-MAIL ☐ OTHER

CONTACT BETWEEN:

CONTACT INITIATED BY:

REASON FOR CONTACT (SUBJECT):

CHILD(REN)'S REACTIONS:

NOTES:

DATE:	TIME:	LENGTH OF CONTACT:

TYPE OF CONTACT: ☐ PHONE ☐ TEXT ☐ VIDEO CALL ☐ E-MAIL ☐ OTHER

CONTACT BETWEEN:

CONTACT INITIATED BY:

REASON FOR CONTACT (SUBJECT):

CHILD(REN)'S REACTIONS:

NOTES:

COMMUNICATIONS RECORD

DATE:	TIME:	LENGTH OF CONTACT:

TYPE OF CONTACT: ☐ PHONE ☐ TEXT ☐ VIDEO CALL ☐ E-MAIL ☐ OTHER

CONTACT BETWEEN:

CONTACT INITIATED BY:

REASON FOR CONTACT (SUBJECT):

CHILD(REN)'S REACTIONS:

NOTES:

DATE:	TIME:	LENGTH OF CONTACT:

TYPE OF CONTACT: ☐ PHONE ☐ TEXT ☐ VIDEO CALL ☐ E-MAIL ☐ OTHER

CONTACT BETWEEN:

CONTACT INITIATED BY:

REASON FOR CONTACT (SUBJECT):

CHILD(REN)'S REACTIONS:

NOTES:

COMMUNICATIONS RECORD

DATE:	TIME:	LENGTH OF CONTACT:

TYPE OF CONTACT: ☐ PHONE ☐ TEXT ☐ VIDEO CALL ☐ E-MAIL ☐ OTHER

CONTACT BETWEEN:

CONTACT INITIATED BY:

REASON FOR CONTACT (SUBJECT):

CHILD(REN)'S REACTIONS:

NOTES:

DATE:	TIME:	LENGTH OF CONTACT:

TYPE OF CONTACT: ☐ PHONE ☐ TEXT ☐ VIDEO CALL ☐ E-MAIL ☐ OTHER

CONTACT BETWEEN:

CONTACT INITIATED BY:

REASON FOR CONTACT (SUBJECT):

CHILD(REN)'S REACTIONS:

NOTES:

COMMUNICATIONS RECORD

DATE:	TIME:	LENGTH OF CONTACT:

TYPE OF CONTACT: ☐ PHONE ☐ TEXT ☐ VIDEO CALL ☐ E-MAIL ☐ OTHER

CONTACT BETWEEN:

CONTACT INITIATED BY:

REASON FOR CONTACT (SUBJECT):

CHILD(REN)'S REACTIONS:

NOTES:

DATE:	TIME:	LENGTH OF CONTACT:

TYPE OF CONTACT: ☐ PHONE ☐ TEXT ☐ VIDEO CALL ☐ E-MAIL ☐ OTHER

CONTACT BETWEEN:

CONTACT INITIATED BY:

REASON FOR CONTACT (SUBJECT):

CHILD(REN)'S REACTIONS:

NOTES:

COMMUNICATIONS RECORD

DATE:	TIME:	LENGTH OF CONTACT:

TYPE OF CONTACT: ☐ PHONE ☐ TEXT ☐ VIDEO CALL ☐ E-MAIL ☐ OTHER

CONTACT BETWEEN:

CONTACT INITIATED BY:

REASON FOR CONTACT (SUBJECT):

CHILD(REN)'S REACTIONS:

NOTES:

DATE:	TIME:	LENGTH OF CONTACT:

TYPE OF CONTACT: ☐ PHONE ☐ TEXT ☐ VIDEO CALL ☐ E-MAIL ☐ OTHER

CONTACT BETWEEN:

CONTACT INITIATED BY:

REASON FOR CONTACT (SUBJECT):

CHILD(REN)'S REACTIONS:

NOTES:

COMMUNICATIONS RECORD

DATE:	TIME:	LENGTH OF CONTACT:

TYPE OF CONTACT: ☐ PHONE ☐ TEXT ☐ VIDEO CALL ☐ E-MAIL ☐ OTHER

CONTACT BETWEEN:

CONTACT INITIATED BY:

REASON FOR CONTACT (SUBJECT):

CHILD(REN)'S REACTIONS:

NOTES:

DATE:	TIME:	LENGTH OF CONTACT:

TYPE OF CONTACT: ☐ PHONE ☐ TEXT ☐ VIDEO CALL ☐ E-MAIL ☐ OTHER

CONTACT BETWEEN:

CONTACT INITIATED BY:

REASON FOR CONTACT (SUBJECT):

CHILD(REN)'S REACTIONS:

NOTES:

COMMUNICATIONS RECORD

DATE:	TIME:	LENGTH OF CONTACT:

TYPE OF CONTACT: ☐ PHONE ☐ TEXT ☐ VIDEO CALL ☐ E-MAIL ☐ OTHER

CONTACT BETWEEN:

CONTACT INITIATED BY:

REASON FOR CONTACT (SUBJECT):

CHILD(REN)'S REACTIONS:

NOTES:

DATE:	TIME:	LENGTH OF CONTACT:

TYPE OF CONTACT: ☐ PHONE ☐ TEXT ☐ VIDEO CALL ☐ E-MAIL ☐ OTHER

CONTACT BETWEEN:

CONTACT INITIATED BY:

REASON FOR CONTACT (SUBJECT):

CHILD(REN)'S REACTIONS:

NOTES:

COMMUNICATIONS RECORD

DATE:	TIME:	LENGTH OF CONTACT:

TYPE OF CONTACT: ☐ PHONE ☐ TEXT ☐ VIDEO CALL ☐ E-MAIL ☐ OTHER

CONTACT BETWEEN:

CONTACT INITIATED BY:

REASON FOR CONTACT (SUBJECT):

CHILD(REN)'S REACTIONS:

NOTES:

DATE:	TIME:	LENGTH OF CONTACT:

TYPE OF CONTACT: ☐ PHONE ☐ TEXT ☐ VIDEO CALL ☐ E-MAIL ☐ OTHER

CONTACT BETWEEN:

CONTACT INITIATED BY:

REASON FOR CONTACT (SUBJECT):

CHILD(REN)'S REACTIONS:

NOTES:

COMMUNICATIONS RECORD

DATE:	TIME:	LENGTH OF CONTACT:

TYPE OF CONTACT: ☐ PHONE ☐ TEXT ☐ VIDEO CALL ☐ E-MAIL ☐ OTHER

CONTACT BETWEEN:

CONTACT INITIATED BY:

REASON FOR CONTACT (SUBJECT):

CHILD(REN)'S REACTIONS:

NOTES:

DATE:	TIME:	LENGTH OF CONTACT:

TYPE OF CONTACT: ☐ PHONE ☐ TEXT ☐ VIDEO CALL ☐ E-MAIL ☐ OTHER

CONTACT BETWEEN:

CONTACT INITIATED BY:

REASON FOR CONTACT (SUBJECT):

CHILD(REN)'S REACTIONS:

NOTES:

COMMUNICATIONS RECORD

DATE:	TIME:	LENGTH OF CONTACT:

TYPE OF CONTACT: ☐ PHONE ☐ TEXT ☐ VIDEO CALL ☐ E-MAIL ☐ OTHER

CONTACT BETWEEN:

CONTACT INITIATED BY:

REASON FOR CONTACT (SUBJECT):

CHILD(REN)'S REACTIONS:

NOTES:

DATE:	TIME:	LENGTH OF CONTACT:

TYPE OF CONTACT: ☐ PHONE ☐ TEXT ☐ VIDEO CALL ☐ E-MAIL ☐ OTHER

CONTACT BETWEEN:

CONTACT INITIATED BY:

REASON FOR CONTACT (SUBJECT):

CHILD(REN)'S REACTIONS:

NOTES:

COMMUNICATIONS RECORD

DATE:	TIME:	LENGTH OF CONTACT:

TYPE OF CONTACT: ☐ PHONE ☐ TEXT ☐ VIDEO CALL ☐ E-MAIL ☐ OTHER

CONTACT BETWEEN:

CONTACT INITIATED BY:

REASON FOR CONTACT (SUBJECT):

CHILD(REN)'S REACTIONS:

NOTES:

DATE:	TIME:	LENGTH OF CONTACT:

TYPE OF CONTACT: ☐ PHONE ☐ TEXT ☐ VIDEO CALL ☐ E-MAIL ☐ OTHER

CONTACT BETWEEN:

CONTACT INITIATED BY:

REASON FOR CONTACT (SUBJECT):

CHILD(REN)'S REACTIONS:

NOTES:

COMMUNICATIONS RECORD

DATE:	TIME:	LENGTH OF CONTACT:

TYPE OF CONTACT: ☐ PHONE ☐ TEXT ☐ VIDEO CALL ☐ E-MAIL ☐ OTHER

CONTACT BETWEEN:

CONTACT INITIATED BY:

REASON FOR CONTACT (SUBJECT):

CHILD(REN)'S REACTIONS:

NOTES:

DATE:	TIME:	LENGTH OF CONTACT:

TYPE OF CONTACT: ☐ PHONE ☐ TEXT ☐ VIDEO CALL ☐ E-MAIL ☐ OTHER

CONTACT BETWEEN:

CONTACT INITIATED BY:

REASON FOR CONTACT (SUBJECT):

CHILD(REN)'S REACTIONS:

NOTES:

COMMUNICATIONS RECORD

DATE:	TIME:	LENGTH OF CONTACT:

TYPE OF CONTACT: ☐ PHONE ☐ TEXT ☐ VIDEO CALL ☐ E-MAIL ☐ OTHER

CONTACT BETWEEN:

CONTACT INITIATED BY:

REASON FOR CONTACT (SUBJECT):

CHILD(REN)'S REACTIONS:

NOTES:

DATE:	TIME:	LENGTH OF CONTACT:

TYPE OF CONTACT: ☐ PHONE ☐ TEXT ☐ VIDEO CALL ☐ E-MAIL ☐ OTHER

CONTACT BETWEEN:

CONTACT INITIATED BY:

REASON FOR CONTACT (SUBJECT):

CHILD(REN)'S REACTIONS:

NOTES:

COMMUNICATIONS RECORD

DATE:	TIME:	LENGTH OF CONTACT:

TYPE OF CONTACT: ☐ PHONE ☐ TEXT ☐ VIDEO CALL ☐ E-MAIL ☐ OTHER

CONTACT BETWEEN:

CONTACT INITIATED BY:

REASON FOR CONTACT (SUBJECT):

CHILD(REN)'S REACTIONS:

NOTES:

DATE:	TIME:	LENGTH OF CONTACT:

TYPE OF CONTACT: ☐ PHONE ☐ TEXT ☐ VIDEO CALL ☐ E-MAIL ☐ OTHER

CONTACT BETWEEN:

CONTACT INITIATED BY:

REASON FOR CONTACT (SUBJECT):

CHILD(REN)'S REACTIONS:

NOTES:

COMMUNICATIONS RECORD

DATE:	TIME:	LENGTH OF CONTACT:

TYPE OF CONTACT: ☐ PHONE ☐ TEXT ☐ VIDEO CALL ☐ E-MAIL ☐ OTHER

CONTACT BETWEEN:

CONTACT INITIATED BY:

REASON FOR CONTACT (SUBJECT):

CHILD(REN)'S REACTIONS:

NOTES:

DATE:	TIME:	LENGTH OF CONTACT:

TYPE OF CONTACT: ☐ PHONE ☐ TEXT ☐ VIDEO CALL ☐ E-MAIL ☐ OTHER

CONTACT BETWEEN:

CONTACT INITIATED BY:

REASON FOR CONTACT (SUBJECT):

CHILD(REN)'S REACTIONS:

NOTES:

COMMUNICATIONS RECORD

DATE:	TIME:	LENGTH OF CONTACT:

TYPE OF CONTACT: ☐ PHONE ☐ TEXT ☐ VIDEO CALL ☐ E-MAIL ☐ OTHER

CONTACT BETWEEN:

CONTACT INITIATED BY:

REASON FOR CONTACT (SUBJECT):

CHILD(REN)'S REACTIONS:

NOTES:

DATE:	TIME:	LENGTH OF CONTACT:

TYPE OF CONTACT: ☐ PHONE ☐ TEXT ☐ VIDEO CALL ☐ E-MAIL ☐ OTHER

CONTACT BETWEEN:

CONTACT INITIATED BY:

REASON FOR CONTACT (SUBJECT):

CHILD(REN)'S REACTIONS:

NOTES:

COMMUNICATIONS RECORD

DATE:	TIME:	LENGTH OF CONTACT:

TYPE OF CONTACT: ☐ PHONE ☐ TEXT ☐ VIDEO CALL ☐ E-MAIL ☐ OTHER

CONTACT BETWEEN:

CONTACT INITIATED BY:

REASON FOR CONTACT (SUBJECT):

CHILD(REN)'S REACTIONS:

NOTES:

DATE:	TIME:	LENGTH OF CONTACT:

TYPE OF CONTACT: ☐ PHONE ☐ TEXT ☐ VIDEO CALL ☐ E-MAIL ☐ OTHER

CONTACT BETWEEN:

CONTACT INITIATED BY:

REASON FOR CONTACT (SUBJECT):

CHILD(REN)'S REACTIONS:

NOTES:

COMMUNICATIONS RECORD

DATE:	TIME:	LENGTH OF CONTACT:

TYPE OF CONTACT: ☐ PHONE ☐ TEXT ☐ VIDEO CALL ☐ E-MAIL ☐ OTHER

CONTACT BETWEEN:

CONTACT INITIATED BY:

REASON FOR CONTACT (SUBJECT):

CHILD(REN)'S REACTIONS:

NOTES:

DATE:	TIME:	LENGTH OF CONTACT:

TYPE OF CONTACT: ☐ PHONE ☐ TEXT ☐ VIDEO CALL ☐ E-MAIL ☐ OTHER

CONTACT BETWEEN:

CONTACT INITIATED BY:

REASON FOR CONTACT (SUBJECT):

CHILD(REN)'S REACTIONS:

NOTES:

COMMUNICATIONS RECORD

DATE:	TIME:	LENGTH OF CONTACT:

TYPE OF CONTACT: ☐ PHONE ☐ TEXT ☐ VIDEO CALL ☐ E-MAIL ☐ OTHER

CONTACT BETWEEN:

CONTACT INITIATED BY:

REASON FOR CONTACT (SUBJECT):

CHILD(REN)'S REACTIONS:

NOTES:

DATE:	TIME:	LENGTH OF CONTACT:

TYPE OF CONTACT: ☐ PHONE ☐ TEXT ☐ VIDEO CALL ☐ E-MAIL ☐ OTHER

CONTACT BETWEEN:

CONTACT INITIATED BY:

REASON FOR CONTACT (SUBJECT):

CHILD(REN)'S REACTIONS:

NOTES:

ADDITIONAL NOTES

ADDITIONAL NOTES

ADDITIONAL NOTES

ADDITIONAL NOTES

ADDITIONAL NOTES

ADDITIONAL NOTES

ADDITIONAL NOTES

ADDITIONAL NOTES

ADDITIONAL NOTES

ADDITIONAL NOTES

ADDITIONAL NOTES

ADDITIONAL NOTES

ADDITIONAL NOTES

ADDITIONAL NOTES

ADDITIONAL NOTES

ADDITIONAL NOTES

ADDITIONAL NOTES

ADDITIONAL NOTES

ADDITIONAL NOTES

ADDITIONAL NOTES

Made in United States
Troutdale, OR
03/07/2025